The Braves' Banner

MWES Writing Anthology
2013-2014

Writing pieces presented by the students of
Mt. Washington Elementary School

Cover artwork by Cameron Chissom, 2nd Grade

BLACK BOX THEATRE PUBLISHING
Copyright © 2014 by Mt. Washington Elementary School

Published by Black Box Publishing Company

ALL RIGHTS RESERVED

CAUTION:
The Braves' Banner MWES Writing Anthology 2013-2014
is fully protected under the copyright laws of the United States of America, and all other countries of the Copyright Union. All rights, including professional, amateur, motion picture, recitation, lecturing, public reading, radio broadcasting, television and the rights of translation into foreign languages are strictly reserved.

The right to photocopy or videotape can be granted only by the author or publisher. In some cases, the author may choose to allow this, provided permission has been requested prior to the action.

No alterations, deletions or substitutions may be made to the work without the written permission of the author.

All publicity material must contain the author's name, as the sole author of the work.

ISBN# 978-0692022306

Printed in the United States of America

Contents

Fables: p. 7

The Bunny and the Worm, by Kylie Hilton — p. 9
3 Baby Pigs, by Pearce Inmon — p. 10
The Dog and the Wolf, by Carson Luttrell — p. 11
The Hurtful Penguin, by Abbie Mann — p. 12
Tom and Jerry Race, by Madison Miller — p. 13
The Hawk that Raced a Rat, by Jaden Smith — p. 14
The Squirrel Who Stole, by Daniel Tharp — p. 15
The Sneaky Worm, by Taylor Young — p. 16

Poetry: p. 17

Winter, by Destiny Castle — p. 19
Spring, by Justice Cox — p. 20
Winter, by Jason Crenshaw — p. 21
Summer, by Nathaniel Goff — p. 22
The Nature of Fall, by Evan Hall — p. 23
Ice Cream, by Avery Hallinan — p. 24
My School and Teacher, by Kaden Hoglen — p. 25
Flowers, by Lakyn Killen — p. 26
Summer, by Ricky Lacefield — p. 27
Summer, by Kahlyn Mattingly — p. 28
Fall, by Christian Miracle — p. 29
Ms. Pinkston, by Elizabeth Monterosso — p. 30
Fall Leaves/Summer, by Adyson Mudd — p. 31
Summer, by Ryan Norbury — p. 32
Summer, by Kadence Owen — p. 33
Snakes Shed in Fall, by Jaython Smith — p. 34
Summer, by Emma Steier — p. 35

Spring, by Zoe Thomas	p. 36
Families, by Maya Willis	p. 37
Spring/Summer, by Hailey Zortman	p. 38

Stories: p. 39

When I Went to Jail, by Dylan Baker	p. 41
The Adventures of Jimmy Bob Jr., by Trenton Coleman	p. 42
Dark Forest, by Sydney Cook	p. 45
The Magic Earrings, by Karley Davis	p. 48
The Time Machine!, by Chloe Duke	p. 50
A Day at the Field, by Blake Dunn	p. 53
When I'm 100 Years Old, by Emily Garrett	p. 55
Did I Just Do That!, by Natalie Griffith	p. 56
The Pig, by Sierra Karner	p. 59
The Sleepover, by Sarah Kincaid	p. 60
Bad X-Mas, by Allyson Lawson	p. 61
Not Home, by Logan Leake	p. 62
Yeehaw, by Ashlee Lewis	p. 63
Three Pups and Ms. Big, by Kelly Lewis	p. 66
Popcorn!!!, by Kendall Mangum	p. 68
One Big Dream, by Jade Meeks	p. 71
Alaskan Survival, by Ethan Mueller	p. 73
Kindle the First, by Alyssa Nourtsis	p. 75
The Super Ninja's Secret Identity, by Cameron Rieber	p. 76
A Giant Who Crushed a Tower, by Christian Schweinhart	p. 78
Mix-Up Adventure, by Zachary Sloan	p. 79
The Prince and the Princess, by Abigail Sneed	p. 81
The Secret Portal, by Jared St. Clair	p. 83

Horseback, by Leslie Steier   p. 84
Bacon!, by Kaden Whicker   p. 86
What the Heck Happened!!!, by Kaden Whicker   p. 88

Narratives: p. 91

Personal Narrative, by Audrey Clarkson   p. 93
Meeting Dez off of Austin & Ally,
by Abbi Crenshaw   p. 94
Polar Bear, by Lilly Leveronne   p. 95
My First Deer, by Cole Netherton   p. 96
!!!My Mom Heather!!!!, by Alyssah Sanders   p. 98
When I Went to Michigan, by Morgan Schock   p. 99
My Epic Trip to Disney World!!!!,
by Tyler Wheatley   p. 100
When My Grandma Died, by Grace Whitworth   p. 102

Fables

The bunny and the worm

By: Kylie Hilton

Once there was a worm who always lied. It was not cool! Because he thinks he's better than some people. One day a pink bunny dug a hole in the mud. After he was Done, the worm said, "I can swim". Show me", said bunny. "It is big ok I lied". It was a bad day.

The moral of this fable is never lie no matter what.

3 Baby Pigs – A Fable

By: Pearce Inmon

Once there was a mom pig. She was giving birth to three pigs but one is mean. He pushed his brother but then his mom came to talk to him. She said, "Son please stop!" So he stopped and played with his pig brothers. My moral is to never push on little kids.

The Dog and the Wolf – A Fable

Carson Luttrell

Once there was a dog that was cute. Once there was a wolf that was sneaky. Sneaky wolf!
One day, the dog was playing with his new toy. Suddenly, the wolf came and popped out of the woods! Then the wolf scratched the gate open and snatched the dog! The dog was never seen again!
The moral of my fable is to keep your animals safe!

The Hurtful Penguin

By: Abbie Mann

Once there was a hurtful penguin that liked to eat fish. One day the penguin saw a fish and he said, "Why are you eating us?" And the penguin said, "I'm sorry. That's what I eat." And they agreed to only eat the dead fish! The moral of this story is to not be hurtful.

The End

Tom and Jerry Race

By: Madison Miller

Once there was a cat that was cheater. One day jerry race tom and jerry race tom all though the home and tom had hammer so jerry runs. They ran but tom had a pan! Jerry ran as then tom hits jerry. Then jerry calls a dog to get tom and that will help jerry to win!

The moral of this fable is you don't cheat or something will hurt!

The hawk that raced a rat

By: Jaden Smith

Once there was a sneaky Hawk. It challenged a rat to a race, the youngest rat, not a baby! That day the rat was practicing and the hawk was sitting down watching his wife feed their babies his wife said "we need more food or our babies will die kill that rat and we will have it for winter". It was the day of the race the hawk was fired up the rat was too. The snake said, "On your mark, get set, go!" swoosh fuse the hawk is gone in one secants the rat too they are both close to the finish line and suddenly the hawk killed the rat in two secants the end! The moral is to not agree with a stranger or you will get hurt.

The Squirrel Who Stole

By: Daniel Tharp

Once there was a squirrel that was hurtful to other squirrel and takes there nuts. Next, the squirrel ran in to a dog and the dog ran the squirrel away. Then the dog ran in to beaver an the beaver chowed down the tree. Last, the dog and the beaver got in a fight and the squirrel watched them fight.

The moral of the fable is to not fight.

The Sneaky Worm

By: Taylor Young

Once there was a worm that was really sneaky. One day the sneaky worm went to the garden and he snuck some cabbage from farmer Dale. Farmer Dale looked down and saw something moving but the worm moved quick enough. When night came, the worm felt really sad about stealing cabbage from famer Dale so he told the truth. The next day the farmer was happy that worm told the truth!

The moral of this fable is to always tell the truth!

Poetry

WINTER

A Haiku by Destiny Castle

I love winter snow.
The snow is white and crunchy.
My foot makes snow crunch.

SPRING

Haikus by Justice Cox

Rain falls, flowers bloom.
Beautiful, bright sun changes all.
Flowers smell sweetly.

The grass is bright green,
Smells fresh, tickles toes and feet.
I love the beautiful breeze.

WINTER

A Haiku by Jason Crenshaw

Snowflakes fall from sky.
I love to go snowboarding.
It's fun to play in snow!

SUMMER

A Haiku by Nathaniel Goff

Swimming in the pool.
I like playing outside.
Playing with my friends.

the nature of fall

By: Evan Hall

icy frost covers
the field , the frost is cold and
rough   here is fall

ICE CREAM

A Haiku by Avery Hallinan

Ice Cream is sweet fun.
I like it—Hope you do, too!
Hope you like all flavors.

MY SCHOOL AND TEACHER

A Haiku by Kaden Hoglen

I love my school and teacher.
Going to miss my teacher,
When I go to 3rd grade.

Flowers

By : Lakyn Killen

Flowers flowers so bright they glow, their thorns are like daggers, my roots are like snakes , my pedals are as smooth as a baby's bottom. And the flowers are so pretty you can't take your eyes of it.

SUMMER

A Haiku by Ricky Lacefield

Summer is so hot!
Summer is really awesome!
Summer is really hot!

SUMMER

A Haiku by Kahlyn Mattingly

I love playing games!
I love playing outside!
We get out of school!

FALL

A Haiku by Christian Miracle

Fall is so much fun,
Because I can rake the leaves.
I jump into leaves.

MS. PINKSTON

A Haiku by Elizabeth Monterosso

Ms. Pinkston is sweet.
Pretty, lovely, can't be beat.
Loving and cheerful.

Fall Leaves

By: Adyson Mudd

Beautiful pumpkins
Autumn leaves blow past my feet
time for hot cocoa

Summer

By: Adyson Mudd

Summer time is here
The sun shines bright on my house
Yay   summer is here

SUMMER

A Haiku by Ryan Norbury

Summer is great play.
I love to be in summer.
Summer is my favorite!

SUMMER

A Haiku by Kadence Owen

Swimming is so fun!
We run and run, all day long.
No school, today. Hurray!

Snakes Shed in Fall

by Jaython Smith

snakes shed in autumn
when they shed their skin it's white
clear and milky pale

SUMMER

A Haiku by Emma Steier

We get out of school.
Light is brightest, you can see.
You'll never be cold.

Spring

by: Zoe Thomas

flowers are blooming
the sun has come out spring's here
let's go play outside

FAMILIES

A Haiku by Maya Willis

Families love and care.
My diary is secret fun.
I love my family.

Spring/Summer

By Hailey Zortman

I love spring
Rain, flowers, and no coat
Warm weather
Play outside
Play in springer
Sunny out
No snow
Thunderstorms
Hurricanes
Play with friends
Swing, slide
Green grass

Stories

When I went to Jail

By Dylan Baker

I went to my friend`s house one day and he said "do you want to go steal a dirt bike because I really wanted a dirt bike. And how Im I going to get in trouble no one is going to see us but after we stole the dirt bike the cop`s showed up! and they said you are going to jail!

I called my mom and dad and told them that I owned the cops 25,000 dollars .My dad said he would pay half and I had to pay the rest.

I could hear people yelling I could thouch the rustey bars I could smell prisoner bad breath I could see prisoners puncing other prisoners.

Then it was my time for lunch all I got was 2 rotten apples .after that I got to talk to my mom therw a glass window it had 10 holes in it so you could hear what they where saying

Then my mom said that she bailed me out I was so happy that I payed the 25,000 dollars my self but I asked my mom if she bailed my friend out she said no then I went over and bailed him out we had lots of fun when he got out and I told the police that I would never steal any thing else

The Adventures of Jimmy Bob Jr.

By: Trenton Coleman

Once upon a time there was a boy named Jimmy Bob Jr. He loved to go on adventures. But this adventure was going to be the strangest one yet.

It all started when Jimmy said to his mom, "I am going to the woods to see if there is something new." His mom said back to him, "All right just do not get in to any trouble."

So Jimmy headed off in to the woods. But when he got there something strange happened there was a flashing light. Jimmy ran home as fast as a cheetah trying to get it's pray. As soon as he got home he said to his mom, "There was a flashing light in the woods. Come look! Come look!"

Mom said, "Jimmy, it was probably your imagination playing tricks on you!" Jimmy said back to his mom, "It was not my imagination playing tricks on me! I know this because I saw it with my two eyes!" So his mom agreed to see if the light was still there.

But when they got there nothing was there. "I swear that this was where the light was."

His mom said, "Jimmy, I told you so it was just your imagination." After they stopped fighting they went back home.

Jimmy thought to himself, I am going back tomorrow but I am going alone. So the next day he went back to the woods and the light was back. He said to himself, "I am not going back home because it might not be here when I get back." So Jimmy walked into the light…when he passed the light it was a large space of land. There were lakes, rivers, streams and water falls. There was even a chocolate fountain, a white chocolate fountain and large candy canes and a small salamander. Jimmy thought that was funny. Then Jimmy said, "I think I have had enough fun for one day." So Jimmy went back the way he came from but the light would not let him go home, but then he saw a humongous butterfly.

Jimmy ran to it as fast as he could before the butterfly got away. When he jumped on it, it flew him across a volcano but not all the way… he fell onto the volcano's crust, then he tumbled the rest of the way down. When he stopped rolling he got back up, he ran to the nearest house and told them to evacuate their village because the volcano was about to erupt. He looked out the house window there was the giant butterfly.

He ran out the door and jumped back on the butterfly it started to fly once more. This time they flew over the Atlantic Ocean when Hurricane Sandy was going on. Good thing he didn't fall into that one. Jimmy took a little nap before he got home. When he woke up he saw the woods that led to his house. Jimmy jumped off the butterfly when he hit land he started to run home when he got there his mom asked Jimmy where he was all day. Jimmy replied, "I was having an adventure of a life time!"

The End

Dark Forest

By: Sydney Cook
Young Authors District Winner 2014

Once upon a time there lived a princess named Sydney and her karate master Colton as a brother. She lived in a beautiful white castle.

One day the whole kingdom gathered in the town square, for the great knight of England was going on a journey and he needed a brave soul to go with him. "By this hour on Thursday night if you want to go on the journey with the great knight of England you must write your name on a piece of paper and put it in this magic bucket. ", said the king.

The next morning the kingdom gathered in the square again. When she got there everybody was jumping, screaming, and waving. Sydney tried to wiggle her way through the rough crowd. Finally a path cleared out. She walked down the path and then she saw what everybody was screaming about.

The great knight of England was there! As everybody got settled in, the knight said, "I'm Cameron the great knight of England." The magic bucket made of stone turned red and spit out a piece of paper. The piece of paper slowly drifted into Cameron's hand. "Sydney Scott." said

Cameron. She slowly walked on until she was face to face with him.

They walked through a field of tall dark green grass to his cabin. "We're leaving tomorrow." he whispered. The next evening they set off for their journey to the dark forest. The forest was known for its towering dark trees and mysterious low voices.

As they came upon the dark forest Cameron stopped. There was a rustle in the bushes beside them. Someone emerged from the bushes. She knew it was a prince. He wore a sparkling crown. The prince crept up behind them and didn't make a peep.

They walked down the mysterious rocky path into a dead end. There were three other paths. Sydney took the middle, the prince took the one on her left, and Cameron took the one on her right. She walked down the path until she felt a hard tug on the side of her arm. She looked over her shoulder.

A ninja in a black mask was there. The ninja ripped off the mask. It was Colton. "We don't have much time so I'll just get straight to the point. Stay away from the prince. ", demanded Colton.

Meanwhile the prince got eaten by a feisty unicorn because he threatened it. The unicorn ripped him and ate him piece by piece. Cameron meanwhile bumped into Colton and then they

found Sydney shivering and hiding in the bushes.
 They traveled back to the castle and lived happily ever after.

The Magic Earrings

By Karley Davis

Once upon a time there was a girl named Elizabeth. She loved to shop. One day when Elizabeth went to the mall she saw these earrings that change colors that 20 dollars and Elizabeth had 50. So she bought a pair. When she put them on she felt like she was flying.

So when she looks down she was no longer on the ground she wasn't even in the mall. Elizabeth was now outside in Keystone Park. So she flew over to a tree held on and took her earrings off. She climbed down the tree and saw her best friend Katie.

"Katie," Elizabeth said. "I just had something weird happen" "what," said Katie. Well I bought these earrings at the mall and they changed colors. So when I put them on I flew out of the mall and into the park. "Well that's weird," said Katie. "I know I want to get rid of them so I don't float up in the air again," said Elizabeth. "Well go throw them into the creek," said Katie.

Maybe a fish will swallow it. Ok come with me then. So Katie and Elizabeth went down to the creek and throw the earrings in. so later that day Katie and Elizabeth went to Keystone Park and went the creek to go fishing then "I think I have something," said Katie. "Is it a big one," said

Elizabeth." "Yah I think so," said Katie. When Katie pulled it up it was huge.

Then they noticed something it was wearing Elizabeth earrings. So when Katie took it off the hook it started to float in the air but they caught it and took the earrings off of the fish and throw it back in the water. So when they got home they built a fire and throw the earrings into the fire and never saw the earrings again.

The Time Machine!

By Chloe Duke

One day there was a girl named Rose that is 12 years old. She has brown hair and brown eyes and is really tan. Rose also has freckles. She was in her basement with her friends Emma, Rachel, and Jade. They were all bored then rose started to talk "Do you guys want to go outside? Or is it too hot" "Its way to hot!" said Emma and all the other girls just nodded. "Ok then do you guys want to do hide and go seek, tag?" asked Rose. "Sure" all the girls said! So then rose got up and went to a wall to count "10,9,8,7,6,5,4,3,2,1, ready or not here I come!" rose yelled. She looked all around the house till she saw a piece of blond hair behind the stairs. "I found you, oh my check it out its some type of map!" rose said pointing to a map that was taped to the stairs! "It's fake, I think it is, just leave it alone." said Emma. "No lets follow it, it isn't that far." Said rose following the map! The girls just watched her then they started to follow her, well they really ran after her! "Rose, are you crazy? We can't follow a map you found in your basement!" yelled jade at the top of her lungs! "Come let's go it just heads to…. Well I don't really know but we can go to wherever it leads because it looks like it is by my house!" said Rose "Fine let's go but it is not going to lead us somewhere!" said Rachel. So then they followed the map till they stopped at the garden. They soon then noticed it was nothing so they walked back then a big machine popped out of the ground!

"What is that?" asked Emma. They soon then knew that they were in the seats and were already buckled up! "What how did we-" she was then cut off when A BIG bang happed!!! They were then in the future. "Wow this is the future, flying cars and different things!" rose said. And what was best about that little trip was that they got to see the future! Then rose pressed a button that made them go to 2019! They got out of the time machine they saw a bunch of people! "Hey" said rose to some guy "Do you know where Rose Greenwell is?" rose asked the man. "Yea she is in school she is going to be a teacher! Well I'm her father!" "Oh…um…when does she get out?" asked rose to her father that was, well older then what she is used to. "She gets out at about in 30 minutes why?" said roses father Wes. "Well I'm from the future and I'm rose in 2014 I'm 12" Said Rose. Wes then got out his wallet and said "smile." Rose smiled and then Wes looked at the pitcher in his wallet then back a few times. "OMG it is I'm so happy, you are so small!" said Wes. "So how old am I?" asked rose "Your 17. Oh and you are in collage because you are so smart that you made it in collage at 17!" said Wes. "We need to get back home your mom will be there any time soon." said Jade to Rose. "Well, can't we stay here I really want to see me?" asked Rose to Jade. "NO we can't stay here we or we will mess up the future!" yelled jade! So they went back in the time machine they were happy to go home but rose was not happy at all. She wanted to see what she looked like. Was she pretty or ugly well she won't know, she will have to wait 5 years!" She was disappointed a lot so she tried to look happy but she didn't do well.

They went home, went in the living room and there was a very pretty girl sitting on the couch! "Who are you?" asked rose "oh my you are so young Rose! I'm rose and I came here in a time machine, I'm 17!" "Wow you are so pretty!" said rose "I even have Racheal, Jade, and Emma here to!" said older rose and 3 girls came out from behind her! So they all had a good time till all of the older kids went away to their right time!

A Day At the field

By: Blake Dunn #5

It was a beautiful summer day at Black Village Park. We just got to the baseball field. We got some snacks & drinks from the concession stand & some very good seats. My little brother Jace is 5. I am 10 my name is Jenna. Jace got popcorn and I got cotton candy. Jace always trough's a fit. So we had to take him to the **BATHROOM,** and let me say this It was **ABSOULTLY DESCUSTING** in there!! Not only that but there was toilet paper **EVERYWHERE**, in the sink, in the stalls, the floors. Everywhere I looked it was **WHITE** but white was somehow Jaces favorite color. So that got him to stop crying. So then we went back to the stadium and there was **SO MANY** people.

    We checked our tickets, "We are in row 1, seats 60-64," said Jenna. OOHHHHHHH everyone said. (Everyone but me). I mean what is so OOHHHHH about it anyways. So we went to sit in our seats. We were squished like grapes. I mean seriously there weren't even any spacers or arm rests like they have at church there. Anyways we had to deal with it.

Then the announcer came on "DUH NUH NUH NUH NUH NUH DUH DUH". "Attion baseball fans are you ready for a fantastical baseball game" the announcer said YEEEAAAAAA!! Everyone shouted. So they started the game. We were there for 2 hours. Later on it was the final pitch we heard the loud **CRACK** of the bat. Then something exiting happened the ball came towards **OUR SEAT.** And then something caught my eye DAD CAUGHT THE BALL, they put him up on the BIG SCREEN.　　　AND THAT NIGHT WAS VERY EXIDING FOR US.

THE END ☺

When I'm 100 Years old…

By Emily Garrett

When I'm 100 years old I will have 3 dogs and 1 cat and I will be a retired singer and retired cheer coach. I will have 4 kids and their names are Jason Jr., Mason, Emma and, Haylee and have 6 grandchildren and their names are Mick, Payton, Parker, Elizabeth, Sarah, mason Jr., and Jon Jr. When I'm 100 years old I will live in Jordon's mansion in Florida with her and I will play bingo, have tea, do karaoke, and neat with Braedyn, Laykn, and Jordan and I will go on vacation with my husband and my friends. I will visit my grandchildren. I will die when I am 900 years old. I will babysit my grandchildren. And I will have a 100,000,000,000 that's is when I'm 100 years old.

Did I Just Do That!

By: Natalie Griffith

"OH, NO!" yelled Nick. "Did I really just break the window?" I have to call Bobby, the window man.

After dialing Bobby's number, a voice answered and said, "Hello. How may I help you?"

"Um, I need bobby to come out here."

"Ok, he will be right over," replied the lady at the front desk.

Later that afternoon there was a knock on the door. "Hi nick" said Bobby. "What is your problem today?"

"I was playing basketball. I thought the ball was going to go in, but instead it hit the window. Please hurry and fix it, because my sister might see me. She will call my mom and I'll get in trouble for it," grumbled Nick.

"Which window?" asked Bobby?

"This one." said Nick.

Just then that tattletale sister of Nick's walked out the door. "Hi Nick," said Katie. "What is Bobby doing here?"

He's just making sure the windows aren't squeaky," lied Nick.

Ok nick! Katie sang as she walked away. "Bye, bye".

"If I get in trouble... Oh well, I won't care," Nick whispered to himself.

"What if they don't figure out that you broke the window?" Questioned Bobby.

"Then that's good for me," bragged Nick.

"Nick you know you're a lucky boy," said Bobby.

"Yah, so are a lot of other kids in the world. Moms home!" yelled Nick.

"Well, hi." said Bobby.

Rhonda, Nick's mom, replied "Hi, Bobby." What is Bobby doing here, Nick?" wondered Rhonda?

"I was going to keep it a secret, but I'll spill the beans. I was playing basketball. I thought the ball was going to make a goal, but instead it rolled off and broke the window," Nick said with an embarrassing look on his face.

"WHAT! Where is the broken window!" hollered Rhonda.

"Its fixed now, Mom." revealed nick.

"Ok, it was a big deal, but I'm happy that you told me," declared Rhonda.

Rhonda looked over at Bobby with an angry face, "Bobby?"

"What? Don't look at me. I didn't do anything," he answered. "Fine, I told your son that I would always keep his secrets."

"Bobby, you are an adult. You should tell me this stuff," complained Rhonda.

"Bobby you know the drill," said Rhonda! I think somebody owes you a little something."

"Do I have to?" whined Bobby.

"Yes, "answered Rhonda.

"Ok, It's fixed now. That would be $50.00 please. Well now... hand it over," Bobby teased Nick in a happy voice.

In the end, Bobby didn't make Nick actually pay him. He was a good friend of the family and liked goofing around with Nick.

The Pig

By Sierra Karner

Mommy, mommy look it's a pig in the yard! Said Jessica.
What a pig in the yard you have to be kidding. Said Riley.
Nope there's really a pig in the front yard. Come look mommy. Said Jessica.
Fine. Oh you weren't kidding were you?
Pig – Oink oink
Well the pig must have-
Pig-oink oink
 Come from –
Pig-oink oink
Well the pig must have –
Pig-oink oink
Come from –
Pig- oink oink
Slow poke farm –
Pig- oink oink
Down the-
Pig- oink oink
STREET!
Pig- Oink Oink
Ha ha pig I got to finish my sentence! Said Riley.
Pig- oink oink

The Sleepover

By: Sarah Kincaid

One day there were 8 girls .One girl had a sleepover. Their names are Kayla, Sarah, Brook, Lilly and Sophia .Sarah and Sophia were best bffs. Everyone is too but Sarah and Sophia are more like BFFS. So, one night Sophia and Sarah went into the woods and Sophia said, "Do you see something red?" Sarah said, "yes." It came closer and closer and closer. Then they ran away. But it was just a girl that had some apples. So they went to sleep. The next day they said, "let's not do that again!"

Bad X-Mas

By: Allyson Lawson

One snowy afternoon Mary Jan was cooking blueberry muffins, oh I mean eating most of them. She was cooking them because she was going to a family gathering at her Aunt Beth's house. She was so happy that she was going to see her family in after so long. Once the muffins where done she tasted one, "Mmmmm these taste AWESOME" Mary said. After Mary was done getting dress, she tried to open her front door it was STUCK! She tried the back door it was STUCK too! Mary called her family to let them know that she wasn't going to make it.

That morning the sun was out. Mary ate her breakfast and watched Vampire Diaries. Mary called a family member to get her door open. When he got there he got a wooden stake and hit it with a hammer. He told her to open the door and it worked. Mary got dressed and left. When she got there she had a fun time. When it was time to leave the door was STUCK!

THE END

Not Home

By: Logan Leake

One day in High Lake, Ohio a seven year old boy named Reed. He was tall, had black hair, and was a light brown tan. He was watching cartoons on his television show. When he overheard his mom Jessie yelling at his dad Joe.

Mom loves to where this perfume that she thought it smelled like flowers to me it smelled like a skunk that just sprayed out the flower he ate earlier. Dad is my favorite parent he lets me stay up longer than mom only when she's not home from work yet and he lets me eat candy mom says it's bad for me. I was still trying to watch cartoons but they were still fighting. So I went to bed I got a headache. The soft blue cover on me helped a lot.

The next day mom came in my room not even knocking on the door. Saying " I have to go to dads" then I knew something was up after she said that there was a knock on the door I rushed to the door it was dad he walked in and told me don't come in mom's room so I didn't. I was wondering what was going on a few minutes later mom came out and told me "you're not going to dads today and you never will" then dad always lived with us forever and ever.

YEEHAW

By: Ashlee Lewis

What could I be doing up at 2:00am? I am riding my horse across the desert trying not to be spotted by the hungry animals. My friends and I are meeting up to explore. Just then we spotted a ghost town. Bradly, John, Travis and I went to check it out. By the way my name is Hunter. Once my friends and I reached the ghost town we heard strange music. Travis and Bradly stood guard while John and I checked out the houses. While John checked the store he sensed the music getting closer, so he called me over to check the Inn. Meanwhile, Bradly and Travis stood guard and heard banging.

"Bradly, Travis, get over here now! We found Skipper!" John and I screamed together.

"No way! We don't believe you. Let us see for ourselves?" They called. As the boys approached the Inn a girl came out from the store and almost took down Hunter.

"Hey, hey don't be so mean we are happy you are here with Skipper," yelled Travis as he also got tackled.

"Well I don't like people barging in my town and making a racket," replied the girl in an angry voice

"Cheyanne, Cheyanne don't be so harsh. They are my friends, even though you are my friend," argued Skipper.

"Is Cheyanne a cowgirl like us?" I whispered to Skipper.

"No, bu-

"No! Why isn't she? She needs to be," I interrupted.

"As I was saying no, but she would like to be if you don't mind," continued Skipper.

"That would be awesome! When we lost you in that town last month, how did you make it here?" I wondered aloud.

"My horse Connor and I wondered until we found this town," replied Skipper.

As I walked over to Cheyanne I felt nervous.

"Um, excuse me Cheyanne but I was wondering if you would like to join my group of cowboys?" I nervously asked Cheyanne.

"Let me think, of course I will!" responded Cheyanne.

"Awesome! Let me tell the others the new," I said excitedly. As I rounded up the rest and told them, Travis asked, "When are we leaving this town? I heard there is a great place about 2 miles from here."

"Travis, it's only 3:00am. Plus we will startle the animals," I replied.

"Fine, fine, but something is so strange about this town. Do you think we are being watched?" remarked Travis.

"No, you are being crazy. Who would want to watch us in a desert ghost town?" I said.

"Is everyone ready to leave and go to the other place?" questioned john.

"We are," replied Cheyanne and Skipper.

"So am I!" Followed Travis.

"I guess I am," I said quietly. As the gang jumped on their horses a pond sparkled in the distance. The horses chased after a lizard to our next place, a farm.

"One day we will make a huge discovery. Today might be the day." Cheyanne remarked

"Halt! Halt!" I screamed as we came to a dead stop.

"What is that huge crack with a river at the bottom?" Travis wondered aloud.

"Nobody knows but, I think we just made a huge discovery." replied Hunter. That is how we know about the Grand Canyon. What else do you think we will find?

Three pups and Ms. Big…

Written by Kelly Lewis

"Hey Cooty and Big Buck do you think its cold out here?" asked Loosy Locket. "Yes, it's a little cold but let's play a little longer" said Cooty. Then Cooty yelped, "Big Buck, toss me that rope." And while the two boy pups were playing Loosy Locket went in there little doggy house.

Eventually the two boy pups went in with Loosy Locket, but in the middle of the night. A massive storm came. It almost tore a tree from the ground by the swing sets in the dog park.

When they woke up they thought what in the world happened!!! Everything was demolished or out of place. Since the storm had done so much to the little dog park. They were eager to find out what else the storm had done.

As they walked Cooty thought he heard something like 'bo bo ba zoo zee za suo.' So Cooty told Loosy Locket and Big Buck about the awkward sound as they turned around the corner.

But right as they turned they knew who that sound was coming from, Ms. Big Witch, The meanest and nastiest witch ever to be seen! Big Buck thought for the first time he was scared. The pups could feel shivers going up their legs by the sight of Ms. Big Witch.

Then suddenly they saw a bridge .They were just about to cross when Ms. Big Witch came and said. No one trespasses my bridge .After that Big Buck demanded to cross the bridge. But Ms. Big Witch said "No"!! That's when the pups thought "that's it! You've crossed the line." So they fought, fought, and fought.

Eventually Loosy Locket stepped up to Ms. Big Witch and politely asked her "can we please pass your bridge?" Ms. Big Witch said, "Yes since you weren't rude this time!" Then Cooty asked can you please fix our park? Ms. Big Witch could just see the depression on his face and she had to fix their home. So she said, "Yes".

Now they all know that you don't get things by being mean but you can get your way if you be nice.

POPCORN!!!

By: Kendall Mangum

Popcorn! I love it so much! I want it day and night! Is it just me or what? The news came on we have breaking news, NO more popcorn, no one likes it! Nooooooo!!!!!!! I wish they made pizza go I HATE pizza!!! What will I do without popcorn? I need to go to my secret popcorn volt. I ran to my room. I looked in my volt… ahhhhhhhhh!!! My popcorn was replaced with pizza! I ran to my sister's room I did the cat eye at her.

"What did you do with my great pizza, I mean popcorn?"

"What in the world are you talking about?"

"I totally hate that food. And you know that. But you love pizza and it's just gross."

I walked out of her room. That smelled like pizza, Yuk! I called my mom to tell her what happened. "Hi mom, THERE IS NO MORE POPCORN!"

"Go buy some then."

"I can't they said everyone hates it."

"What will I do? I can't do anything."

"I know what you can do. Drive me to the factory pleases with a cherry on top."

"Fine, but wait until I come home. I will be home as fast as I can."

"COME HOME NOW!!!" I put the phone down someone came to the door I looked out the door it was my sister friend. I opened the door she said, "Can I see your sis do you have popcorn?"

"No, my friend does though."

"Man… wait can you tell me where he lives."

"It's a girl!" I knew that but I will let you in to see my sis ok. He lives down the street. Now let me in. fine. I let her in. I walked down the street where she told me to go. I knocked. She came.

"Do you have any popcorn?"

"Yeah so what if I have popcorn."

"I Need It Now!"

"Ok I will tell you where I store the popcorn. IN MY FACTORY!! But… you don't get any."

"But I love popcorn!"

"So I make it and you don't make the rules here." She slammed the door on my arm.

GRRRR. That hurt bad. Now what! I totally can't live without popcorn! I ran to my mom she finally came home! She said she would drive me there. I hopped in the car and we left. We drove down the streets where the mean girl's place is.

"Wait, where are we going?"

"To the girl that owns the factory."

"I know that I just went there, she is totally mean with a with capital M."

"It's our only chance," I told her to go up there no one answered. My mom came and told me no one's home. I ran out of the car in to the house and into my room. My sister's friends heard me crying.

"She gave me the key to the factory."

"Yay! You have the key and you're giving it to me wow!"

"No problem. I don't need it."

I got on my bike and zoomed to the factory. I unlocked it… popcorn was everywhere. I say, "There are over one million or more! AHHHHHH!!!!!!! I love it so much!" My sis walked in, I hit her because she touched the popcorn. I love it and no one can touch it or I will bite you if you were like popcorn then I would eat you!

One Big Dream

By Jade Meeks

It's big its round you can play with it, it's as black lines you dribble it you bounce it you pass it. You see team on television you probably know what it is, it's a basketball.

Hey I am a girl, short as people know for my age I am four feet and four inches. I am in fourth grade my name is Emma I am a point guard. I love basketball but some people don't believe that I can make a girls NBA team or a college team. They say that I short but I don't let it go to my head.

I play for a team name East 4th grade on the team we vs says look at that short girl on the team I prove them wrong because I am a starter for the team I some time make 4 to 6 a game. So I had a game yesterday and went on the court for the first quarter I was the leader kind of, that are in so I got the tip pass the basketball to my sister and she shoot the ball and made it. Any way it was Premiere ball, and they went up the court and they shoot the ball and miss I got the rebound and went for a left hand layup and made it and somebody fowl me so I got the hit free throws 2 I made one and miss one.

So the point people think that I am too short I tell them you see I have a dream that it I want to grow up and be a basketball player I am not going let my dream down so you can think that and I just walk away.

Alaskan Survival

By Ethan Mueller

I live in Alaska with my four brothers: Owen, Eli (Elijah), Liam, Heath and finally, me, Ethan. Liam and Heath go fishing while Owen goes out to help me hunt. Dad cuts our trees (there`s only four months of summer, so most of the time it`s FREEZING) and Mom cares for the cows and horses.

I woke up this morning and heard a deer call, so I got my stuff (bottle of toothpicks, pistol, rifle, knife, camouflage vest, bow and thirty nine arrows) opened the door.... and slammed it shut! Why do I see a Kodiak bear? There`s a trapdoor on the roof. I got the ladder and climbed out: Ready, aim… fire!!!!!!! What's going on? My brothers heard BBBBGGGGRR!! I came in. I told my brothers to get their pistols because I think I got a browny (brown bear). We went outside to investigate........and I got him!! That`s enough food to last three months.

I went out to help Dad with the fire wood, we spent three hours at work, and when I went back I realized Liam and Heath weren't home. It was getting dark, so I got my stuff, went to Cariboo Lake and went to search.

It was the dead of night when I finally found Liam and Heath. I was starving when I got home and I saw a wolf attempting to get to the cattle. He was getting in, so I shot at him and just barely got him in the leg. I reloaded, shot again and he fell. I went to check it out and saw I only broke his leg, so I took him in to heal. When the coyote was healed I secretly led the coyote into the woods and he took off. That's how you get through a day in Alaska.

Wohwohwooooh

Kindle the first

By Alyssa Nourtsis

Once upon a time in a castle in the magical land of rainbow fairies, there lived a girl named Kindle. She is nice. She lives with her parents Kevin and Maggy. They are very nice. They are in bed. Before they know it, Seatrick is trying to trap Kindle and Maggy because he does not like them. Kevin tries to save them by running with five knifes in his hands but it doesn't work now Kevin is trapped too. Kindle screeched "get me out of here"! "No", said her mother. Kindle said, "can I go to bed". "No" said her mother "we are trapped" said her mother. Kevin wants his family but they are 20 miles away. They got the key. They are free they are finding Kevin and unlocking his trap. He is out! They lived happily ever after.

The Super Ninja's Secret Identity

By Cameron Rieber

A long time ago there was a boy named Dragon. He went to middle school.

One day Dragon was in class but every one aggravated him. Dragon was working on a math test. Jacob, the mean boy in class, drew the wrong answer with pin on his paper.

Jacob got in trouble because Dragon told his teacher, Mrs. Dixon and Dragon always tells the truth.

Dragon had a secret. Dragon was a ninja!

Later that night when the sun went down, his mom told Dragon to go to bed, but he didn't. Instead he put on his ninja suit because Mr. Cool, the nation's most feared villain, was out causing trouble.

Dragon and Mr. Cool meet at the museum. They had a ninja fight! Dragon hit Mr. Cool ten times, but Dragon never got hit back. Of course, Mr. Cool lost.

After Dragon came home, he went to bed but he couldn't sleep because he couldn't quit thinking about Mr. Cool. "Oh, gosh! I can't quit thinking about that evil villain! It seems like I've seen him before!"

The next morning after the sun came up, Dragon met Jacob at school. That is when Dragon finally realized that Jacob is Mr. Cool!

Dragon decided to tell Jacob his secret. He was a ninja too! "Jacob, let's be buddies and work together on the same side." said Dragon. "Ok let's be friends!" Jacob replied.

A Giant Who Crushed A Tower

By: Christian Schweinhart

Once upon a time, there lived a giant named Nathan. "Hi! My name is Nathan!", he said. He was mean and destructive!! He'd never been nice to others! He was right by a castle. The time was 5:00 pm. When he was walking by, he wanted to crush the castle. And when he was walking to crush the castle he said, "I hope there's not any buildings behind the castle." There's a tower behind it! The tower was shaking!!!!!!!! And then it collapsed on to the castle!!!!!!!!!!!!!!!! Now the people are very, very mad at Nathan. And Nathan ran home crying!!!!!!!!!!! A week later, Nathan decided to be nice and help rebuild the tower and the castle. And they lived happily ever after. The end

Mix-up Adventure

By Zachary Sloan

Hey Joe my movie is starting on TV. Yea I can't believe that my dad is Indiana Jones. Yea I know I'm grate it is to bad that I am 63 years old or I would make a new move. Hey you don't I do it. Because it is to digress! To bad I am already living tomorrow my cameo man is come to pike me up in the morning! Fine your lose. What you love the jungle that is whir I am going. Ho I am sorry that changes everything. Rill. No it is cold sarcasm! So you are afraid of a set or is it the spiders and scorpion. No whirs unhealthy food bars but the other thing too. Why can't I go! Go to your room we will talk about in the morning! But it is only 9:00 a.m. Ho still go to your room. But don't come crying to me when you need a comeback. What. It was under your name but you know what regret it. What how could you. Simple I go but say that I am not you. Ok you can go. Thank you I will never forget this. I am sure you won't. Ok good night. Wait what time is it. 9:00 p.m. we have been arguing that. Yea why…ho yea I should go to bed now. Ok don't let the bed bugs bit. Wait we have bed bugs. No well maybe. I think I well sleep down here. Ok the widows are down here. ok I think I well sleep on top of the ice box with the dust mite. Ok grab me a sank too. You saw threw that. Yepa you are as big as a hippo.hey w at is that subplots mean. nothing am just kidding you are as thin as a pencil. I am I have been cutting down on snacks. It sure is working *coghno* ho by the way are you looking for. What is ruefully you're the golden tom-a-Hauk. That old thing I have it right here. So we have been arguing for no risen. Yap.

The Prince and the Princess

By Abigail Sneed

Once upon a time there was a prince and a princess that lived in a pink castle. One day the prince had to leave the kingdom to go to an important meeting in another kingdom called kingdom of crazy. So the prince had to leave the princess so she could still she her family. So the prince kissed his princess and left.

The princess went up to her room. Then all the sudden she heard a knock on the door. "Who could that be" said the princess. It was the prince of crazy kingdom to pick up the prince. But the prince did not know the prince of crazy kingdom was coming to pick him up. So the prince of crazy kingdom left. Then then princess went back inside the castle. In front of her stood a big, hairy monster. She was so scared she said "get out of my castle your scary". And just like that the monster left.

The next day the prince returned. She said "I'm so happy to see you" .Then she told her prince everything that happened .He said "really" she said "well do expect me to make all this up? "He said "no I don't expect you to make all

The next day the prince and the princess got out of bed and went down stairs. The princess was worried the monster had returned but he didn't .Later that day the prince and the princess went to kingdom crazy and apologized for the mix up in transportation. The prince of crazy kingdom said "its ok it happens". So the prince and the princess went back home and lived happily ever after.

The end

The Secret Portal

Jared St. Clair

One day in Josh's closet he found a secret room. He went to his dresser and got a flashlight. Then he went in the room.

When he got in the room he saw a box that said portal. After that Josh called his friend over. When Josh told Bob about the box he was so surprised. "Let's open it," Said Bob.

"No that's a terrible idea," Said Josh.

"Ok," Said Bob

After that the two boys told Josh's mom about the room and the box that says portal. They all went back to Josh's room and into the room in his closet. After that Josh's mom opened the box and a purple portal came up that said future in bold red letters. When the three of them went in there they saw robots and flying cars everywhere

Then a robot came up and said, "I want to kill you."

"Go back in the portal," said Josh's mom. "Shut the box," said Josh

Now Josh, Bob, and Josh's mom were glad to be home. They will not open that box again. Well at least for a little while. For now they are all happy.

Horseback

By: Leslie Steier

Once there was a little girl named Hana. She had a horse named Cloe and they went on a trail ride. Hana's long brown hair and Cloe's long brown mane flew with the wind as they dashed through the woods.

They ignored the lightning storm and followed the dirt trail.

The clouds got even darker. They were trotting and almost home when lightning struck the tree close to them. Then Cloe kicked Hana off and ran away far into the woods.

The tree caught fire even though it was raining. Hana zoomed home. She called 911 and led the firemen to the tree. Hana and her family went home worrying about Cloe.

"What happened?" Mom said.

"Can we talk about this in the morning?" said Hana.

Dad heard the fear in Hana's words and replied "That is a great Idea".

"Good night Mom and Dad" Said Hana.

The next morning Hana's family made a plan to hand out flyers and help find Cloe. "She is never going to come back" cried Hana.

"Never say never" Mom responded.

The phone rang. Hana answered it. "Did you find my horse?" asked Hana.

"No, but I did see the flyer." It was Aunt Onna. She was wondering if she could help.

"Can she please, Mom." asked Hana.

Mom said, "Yes."

"YAY!!!" screamed Hana.

Aunt Onna showed up with her horse trailer the next day. "Maybe she brought one of her horses" Hana said.

Aunt Onna got out of her truck, opened the horse trailer and…

Out stepped Cloe!!!!

"THANK YOU!!!!!" squealed Hana. She got on Cloe bare backed and took her to her stall.

"How did you do it?" Mom inquired.

"I have my ways." said Aunt Onna.

Hana went to go give Cloe food and water later that night. It was a stormy night. The next morning…

Cloe was gone! "Here we go again!!" Hana said.

Bacon!

By Kaden Whicker

"BACON!!!!!" Hi I'm Baco, also I'm a dog by what I said you can tell....1. I'm a talking dog. 2. I love bacon.

The reason why I just said bacon well... here's what happened. I was just searching through the channels on the t.v. and then someone on the news said, "Do you love the sweet juicy food bacon? If you do well too bad it's been cancelled," and that's when I started to whimper "Bacon!!!"

My owner Logan heard me howling and whimpering "bacon", while he was heating up some beans. He came in wondering what was wrong

I said to him, "I'm sorry bro we lost her"
Logan replied "My grandmother? Whhhy!!!"
"No, much worse... Bacon," I said.

Then we both started sobbing. Both of us were wondering how we could prevent this.

Ding! That's the sound of a light bulb going off in my head. I have an idea. So I turned the t.v. back on to see where the news was broadcasting. I was in luck because it was just downtown.

Ok we're here...4:55. We got up on stage and I asked, "Who thinks bacon should be cancelled? No one, okay, then why is bacon being cancelled?" Then a pig in a suit and glasses came on stage with us.

"Ahem," the pig said, "Hi, I'm Pigston the 3rd and I don't know what these amateurs are doing up-"

Baco cut him off, "Amateurs! Who you calling amateurs!? I eat bacon raw too!"

Pigston replied, "Did I say amateurs, I-I mean fine gentlemen. The reason why bacon has been cancelled is because there's not that many smart pigs. So they thought when someone comes to get them they thought it's going to be the most fun thing you could ever do. But I was the smart one and the fattest. So I knew soon I was going to be delicious bacon."

Baco cut in again, "But you'd be making people happy?"

Pigston replied, "No, I still have things in life I want to do like play basketball. The point is pigs are people too. Plus what if you were me, would you like to be killed just for food? I don't think so!"

The dog, Baco and the pig, Pigston started arguing. Then Logan yelled,
"ORDER, ORDER!!! Order in the park I have an idea… how about we make bacon out of other animals like cows, good?"

Pigston and Baco mumbled, "Ok." Then they shook paw to hoove.

Three months later…"Bacon!!!" on the t.v. instead of a pig it was the singing cow in the shower from the milk commercial.

"AHOOOO!" the dog howled.

What the Heck Happened!!!

By: Kaden Whicker

"I'm a little fishy, fishy, fishy. I'm a little fishy swimming in the sea… OH MY GOSH, I'M A FISHY WISHY WHAT THE HECK HAPPENED? Hi, didn't see you there as you can tell I'm a fish I guess. You might want to cover your ears. I'M A FISH? WHY ME? Ok it's just, it's just a dream. Someone pinch me."

"Ok, pinch."

"OW! Wait a second another second and another, oh the whole world is fish world. WAIT.WHAT!!! It's not just me well I guess it's better than it being just me."

Some random guy came up to me and said, "Dude why are you talking to yourself?"

"It's a monologue now where were we? Oh right, why did this happen?! It was probably something that was in our food like fish food. Probably eating people food will turn us back to normal, hope so. Here I go crunch… bleh, that tasted terrible and that was cake!!! Sooo now wh-"

What does the fox say? Ring a Ring a Ring…What does…

"Hello, yes, ok, yeah, bye. Hallelujah!!! The reason why I just said that is because my friend Ryan realizes the world is fish world too. Now I need to go see him be right back… And I'm back here's Ryan."

"Sup," Ryan said.

"Now how are we going to turn everybody back?"

"How about we eat some people food?"

"Already tried that," I replied

"Then I'm allllll ouuut…"

"Yeah he's very chill. Now back to my problem. How are we supposed to turn everybody back?"

"Dude, why are you talking to yourself?" Ryan said.

"AGAIN IT'S A DANG MONOLOGUE!!!"

"Ok sheesh, just asking."

"Soooooooo. Oh, I got it let's go to the daca alpaca oh who cares about the dang name we got a world to save or fish bowl whatever, let's go…"

I was panting like a dog when I got there and said, "Whew, that's a work out!" I had to throw a bone to get Ryan to come? (He's kind of like a dog, or fish dog for that matter.) "Now here boy, here," I held up a bone.

Ryan howled, "Awwwoooo."

"What did I do? Oh I'm on your fin, sorry. Now help me figure out what to do."

"Like…what's the magic word?" Ryan said. (And he's back to chill.)

"The machine had two settings, You or Everyone. I put it on YOU, now push, errrrrrrr. Awwwww, man I have little baby fish arms.

"Oh Ryan, here boy!"

I held up a bone and Ryan came. Then I said "Ryan push the pretty switch." Then I thought if it's just him who gets turned back, he'll drown. So quickly I yelled, "Wait!!!"
Then he made that sound like a dog does whenever they're confused and tilted his and said, "Arruu?"
Then I said, "Put it on everyone," and then, push. "Halleluiah!!! We're all back!"

Ryan said, "That's gnarly dude. I'm awesome!" I said back to him, "You're awesome??? I'm the one who had the idea of how to turn us back, son." (F.Y.I. he's not really my son.)
Then he whimpered like a dog and gave me the puppy eyes and I'm a sucker for the puppy eyes even though he's human.

The End

Narratives

Audrey Clarkson   January 30, 2014
1st grade

Personal Narrative

Hello I want to tell you an amazing part of my life. It's when my baby brother was born. My baby Brother was born at Norton suburban hospital and my whole family was there. My mommy was scheaguled for a C/section on November 13 20, 12. Ryder Emerson was born at 11:59 he weigh 8 pounds and two ounces he was 20.5 inches long. I had to wait in the waiting room and then my daddy came out of the surgery room and brot me in there and I saw my brother. I felt really happy that I became a big sister. I was filed with happy, nice.

Meeting Dez off of Austin and Ally

By Abbi Crenshaw

I metted Dez off of Austin and Ally I was excited I have never meet a pop star ever!!!

I meet dez in Tennessee at the aquarium. It was in the afternoon. I was scared and also excited I also sall he had a blue jacket on. I heard him say hi to me I said," hi back in a mumble voice. I touched his coat it was cotton. After I went to Dixie stampede I sall him there. After the horse show at Dixie stamped a bunch of girl's came running to him I went where he could sign my ticket. My mom talked to the parson that drived dez and then we went back to the loge and went to something else. It was so awesome. Maybe you can meet dez at the aquarium if you watch Disney channel maybe you know who he is also nice and funny.

    He loves to be funny. He's hair color is orange. He is not as silly then his character on the show. I learned that day that meeting a super star is like meeting a parson.

Lilly Leveronne 1. 24.14
1st grade

Polar bear

First we need to learn about polar bears .
First some live in Antarctica or the north pole.
They live on the ice and snow. Polar bears eat
fish, walrus pups, and seals. They hunt for thar
pray. Sometimes they dive into the water. Babies
are born toothless, hairless, and blind. They hunt a
lot. I am glad I got to tell you about polar bears.
polar bears.

My First Deer

By: Cole Netherton
Young Authors District Runner Up 2014

It was around 6 o'clock in the evening. There was white snow on the ground. You could see little greenish brownish pieces of grass poking through. When I first saw the deer, it popped out of the woods. It came out of a creek. It was a light brown, the color of root beer. It was eating corn. Birds were eating the corn too.

I was shaking. I was afraid I wasn't going to hit him. I had buck fever. Your heart beats fast and you can't control it. I was taking a deep breath. I heard myself breathing. I had to keep it down so the deer didn't get spooked. I was breathing cold air and I could see a white fog coming from my mouth. The cold brittle wind hurt my face. My cheeks were as red as a sun burn.

I slowly pick up my gun. The cold plastic was brutal to my cheek when I placed it in position on my shoulder. It was heavy. My Pap unlocked the safety. I stared through the scope. My heart was pumping even faster. I took another deep breath so I wouldn't shake the gun. I pulled the trigger and CLICK! Then nothing. CLICK! And then I shot again.

Finally a shot went right through the deer. It fell silently right in its tracks. My Pap was happy for me. He patted my back and giggled as he told me, "Good job." I will always remember my first deer because it hangs on my wall as a trophy to me.

!!!My Mom Heather!!!!

By: Alyssah Sanders

She is a tall beautiful older lady. She has light brown hair that is curly. My mom has light brown eyes. She is a girley girl like me. MY mom likes to wear pretty and gorgeous clothes, she also likes to wear lots of make-up. She is peach and white too!

FIRST, she is a loving lady. She gives hugs& kisses to me. She is a nice mom & she is an encouraging young lady who always cheers me on to try new things.

SECOND, my mom is caring to all. My mom is there for me when I am sick. My mom helps when I am hurt. My mom helps me when I am very sad.

FINALLY, MY mom Heather is a loving young lady that is loving & caring to me. My mom is a one of a kind. She is very special to me.

THE END!!!!!!

When I Went to Michigan

By: Morgan Schock

It took me four hours to get to Michigan! In the middle of the trip, my mom and dad said, "You can get a big bag of donuts and apple juice." I was hungry! Once we got there, I looked around the cabin. I was surprised because my bedroom was upstairs. There were apple trees and a lot of them. Everything was so small. At night it was cold, scary, and dark. There were lots of owl sounds. The hiking trails were very very short because bears and other creepy animals. There was a spider on the shower curtain. My dad squished it under the plunger! I felt very safe! That night, I dreamed about that spider! I will maybe go back.

My Epic Trip to Disney World!!!!

By: Tyler Wheatley

One awesome morning I woke up and my dad said," pack your bags. 'So I said, Ok.'' So a couple of minutes later we headed to the airport because we were going to **Disney World!!!** I was so excited because I have never been to Disney world before or I have never been on a plane before. When we arrived we took a bus to are hotel it was called All Star Movies. When we got to our room we unpacked are bags. Then we headed to Down Town Disney. We explored a while then we went back to are hotel. We put on are bathing suits and went down to the pool and swam. Later that night we went to grab something to eat. I thought it was delicious. That next morning we woke up and went to a park called Magic Kingdom the main park. It was a blast I was having an awesome time. That night we went back down to are hotel and we went down to the pool it was a blast. The next morning we went to Hollywood Studios. It was scary riding tower of terror, but that night we watched an awesome water show called fantasmic. That night we went back to Down Town Disney, and bought some stuff like t-shirts and water bottles. Then we went to the pool to watch a little show. That next day we went to animal kingdom I did not like Animal Kingdom because I was board all day there. The next day is my favorite it's Epoct it was fun going to Epcot because I got to ride Soren, test Track and a boat ride in Mexico. The next day we went to Magic Kingdom. I had a blast but I was also sad because we were leaving the next day. Then we got to are hotel and went to bed because the next day we were leaving. Then that next morning, we woke up and packed to get ready to leave then we went down to the pool then we changed and got on a bus to go to the airport and got ready to take off but are plane got delayed and we finally took off and we landed at Atlanta and ran through the airport because we were going to miss are flight. Then that plane got delayed because of mechanical problems then they put us on that plane and then they took us off that plane. So then we had to go and wait 2 and a half hours for another pilot to come than we took off and landed at Louisville airport and we got in a taxi and arrived home at 5:30 in the morning. I didn't wake up until 1:00 pm. That is the end of my story I hoped you liked it and this doesn't happen to you, but I had an awesome, epic and terrific time at Disney World!!!

The End!!!!!!

When My Grandma Died

By: Grace Whitworth

On December 7th my grandma died. Her name was Virginia Golfenet. She died of lung cancer. The year she died was 2013. I bet she is in a better place called heaven. I think she died a month after I got my kitty. She liked singing and dancing to the 90s music. She always said "yes Virginia, there is a Santa Claus but I don't remember why. I always pray to the Lord wondering how she's doing. The last time I saw her was Thanksgiving. That day I hugged her and almost started to cry because she looked sick in her eyes and how skinny she was. I remember Virginia wanted to stay alive one more Thanksgiving and she did. She may not be on earth this very day but always in my heart. Now that my story is done I just want to say I will always have my grandma in my memory.

The End

NOW AVAILABLE!!!

Poop Happens!" in this send up of all things cowboy!

So, Who Was That Masked Guy Anyway? is the story of Ernie, the grandson of the original Masked Cowboy, a lawman who fought for truth, justice and the cowboy way in the old west. Now that Grandpa is getting on in years he's looking for someone to carry on for him. The only problem? Ernie doesn't know anything about being a cowboy. He's never seen a real cow, he's allergic to milk and to tell the truth he doesn't know one end of a horse from another! So it's off to cowboy school to learn the basics of cowboyology. He'll learn to rope and ride, chew and spit and to develop the perfect "Yee-Haw!". And it's a good thing, because a band of no good outlaws have captured the good people of Gabby Gulch and the President of the United States, Theodore Roosevelt! Now it's up to Ernie and his friends to save the day...but beware, before it's all over, the poop is sure to hit the fans!

NOW AVAILABLE!!!

WANTED: SANTA CLAUS is the story of what happens when a group of department store moguls led by the greedy B. G. Bucks decide to replace Santa Claus with the shiny new "KRINGLE 3000", codenamed...ROBO-SANTA! A new Father Christmas with a titanium alloy outer shell housing a nuclear powered drive train, not to mention a snow white beard and a jolly disposition! These greedy tycoons will stop at nothing to get rid of jolly old St. Nick. That includes framing him for such crimes as purse snatching, tire theft and...oh no...not.....puppy kicking??!! Say it isn't so Santa! Now it's up to Santa's elves to save the day! But Santa's in no shape to take on his stainless steel counterpart! He'll have to train for his big comeback. Enter Mickey, one of the toughest elves of all time! He'll get Santa ready for the big showdown! But it's going to mean reaching deep down inside to find "the eye of the reindeer"!

NOW AVAILABLE!!!

At the edge of the universe sits The Long John Cafe. A place where the average guy and the average "Super" guy can sit and have a cup of coffee and just be themselves...or, someone else if that's what they want. The cafe is populated by iconic figures of the 20th Century, including cowboys, hippies, super heroes and movie stars. They've come to celebrate the end of the old Century and the beginning of tomorrow! That is, if they make it through the night! It seems the evil Dr. McNastiman has other plans for our heroes. Like their total destruction!

NOW AVAILABLE!!!

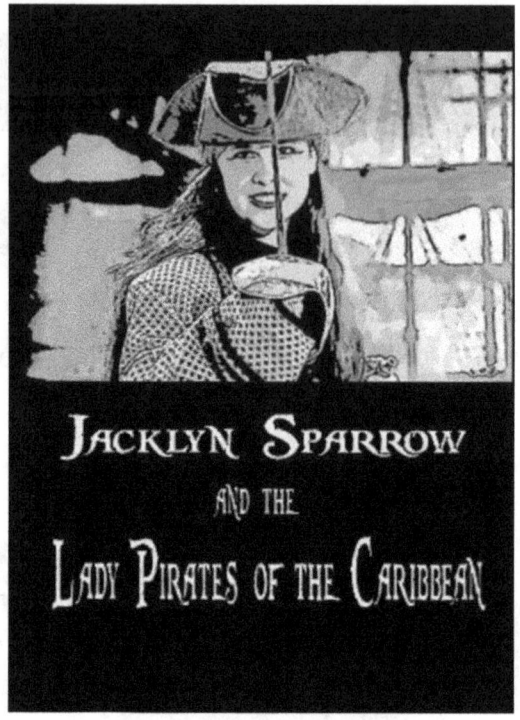

Why should the boys get to have all the fun?

Jacklyn Sparrow and the Lady Pirates of the Caribbean is our brand new swashbuckling pirate parody complete with bloodthirsty buccaneers in massive sword clanking battle scenes!! A giant wise cracking parrot named Polly!! Crazy obsessions with eye liner!! And just who is Robert, the Dreaded Phylum Porifera??

Of course the whole thing ends with a large celebration where everybody gets down with their bad selves!! It's fun for the whole family in this lampoon of everything you love about pirates!!!

NOW AVAILABLE!!!

"May the Dwarf be with you!"

A wacky take on the classic fairy tale which will have audiences rolling in the floor with laughter!

What happens when you mix an articulate mirror, a conceited queen, a prince dressed in purple, seven little people with personality issues, a basket of kumquats and a little Star Wars for good measure?

Snow White and the Seven Dwarves of the Old Republic!

NOW AVAILABLE!!!

Dear John
An ode to the potty.

"My dreams of thee flow softly.
They enter with tender rush.
The still soft sound which echoes,
When I lower the lid and flush."

They say that porcelain is the best antenna for creativity. At least that's what this cast of young people believe in Dear John: An ode to the potty! The action of this one act play takes place almost entirely behind the doors of five bathroom stalls. This short comedy is dedicated to all those term papers, funny pages and Charles Dickens' novels that have been read behind closed (stall) doors!

Bathroom humor at its finest!

NOW AVAILABLE!!!

Declassified after 40 years!

On December 21, 1970, an impromptu meeting took place between the King of Rock and Roll and the Leader of the Free World.

Elvis Meets Nixon (Operation Wiggle) is a short comedy which offers one possible (and ultimately ridiculous) explanation of what happened during that meeting.

NOW AVAILABLE!!!

𝕰𝖛𝖊𝖓 𝕬𝖉𝖆𝖒

In the beginning, there was a man.
Then there was a woman.
And then there was this piece of fruit...
...and that's when everything went horribly wrong!
Even Adam is a short comedy exploring the relationship
between men and women right from day one.

Why doesn't he ever bring her flowers like he used to?
Why doesn't she laugh at his jokes anymore?
And just who is that guy in the red suit?
And how did she convince him to eat that fruit, anyway?

NOW AVAILABLE!!!

Count Dracula is bored. He's pretty much sucked Transylvania dry, and he's looking for a new challenge. So it's off to New York, New York! The Big Apple! The town that never sleeps...that'll pose a challenge for sure.
Dracula purchases The Carfax Theatre and decides to put on a big, flashy Broadway show...

THE DRACULA SPECTACULA!

Of course the Theatre just happens to be across the street from Dr. Seward's Mental Hospital where people have been mysteriously dying since The Count moved in.
Just a coincidence?
The play features a large cast of zany characters and is equal parts horror story and Broadway show spoof!

NOW AVAILABLE!!!

THE FOUR PRESIDENTS examines the lives and characters of four of the most colorful personalities to hold the office. Much of the dialogue comes from the Presidents' own words.

THE FARMER WHO WOULD BE KING presents George Washington through his own words, and the words of his biographer Mason Locke Weems. Was the father of our country a simple farmer who answered the call of his countrymen, or something more?

THE GREAT EMANCIPATOR is the story of a simple man. Born in the wilds of Kentucky and mostly self taught, Abraham Lincoln would someday be regarded as the greatest American who ever lived.

THE BULL MOOSE who occupied the White House 100 years ago was truly a man of action. Theodore Roosevelt was a father, author, rancher, sportsman, policeman, Rough Rider, cowboy, big game hunter, Governor of New York and eventually The President of the United States!

NIXON AND THE GHOSTS is a surreal drama with dialogue ripped straight from the headlines. On the night before his resignation, Nixon ponders his rise and fall, as the shadows themselves seem to come alive and he is confronted by the spirits of Presidents past!

NOW AVAILABLE!!!

The lights rise on a beautiful sunset.
A mermaid is silhouetted against an ocean backdrop.
Hauntingly familiar music fills the air.
Then...the Lawyer shows up.
And that's when the fun really begins!
The Little Mermaid (More or Less.) is the story of a Theatre company attempting to stage a children's version of the Hans Christian Anderson classic. The only problem? It looks and sounds an awful lot like a movie of the same name. That's when the Lawyer for a certain "mouse eared company" starts talking lawsuit for copyright infringement.
Lawsuit?
Copyright infringement?
Throw out the costumes!
What's that? There's a bunch of old clothes backstage from the 1970's? Well, don't just stand there! Go get them!
Ditch the music!
What? Somebody's mom has a greatest disco hits cd out in the car? That'll be perfect!
Change everyone's names!
Tartar Sauce! Little M.! The Crab Formerly Known as Sebastian!
Everybody ready? Ok...Action!!!

NOW AVAILABLE!!!

Adventure has a new name...

CINDERELLA!!!

Cinderella and the Quest for the Crystal Pump, is the story of a young girl seeking a life beyond the endless chores heaped upon her by her grouchy stepmother and two stepsisters.

Mow the grass! Beat the rugs! Churn the buttermilk!

Sometimes it's more than one girl can take!
More than anything, Cinderella wants to go to the prince's masquerade ball, but there's one problem...she has nothing to wear! Luckily, her Fairy Godperson has a few ideas.

Meanwhile, Prince Charles Edward Tiberius Charming III, or "Charlie" as he prefers to be called, has run away with his pals, Touchstone the Jester and the Magic Mirror, searching for a quiet place where he can just enjoy a good book!

Now this mismatched quartet find themselves on a quest to find the greatest treasure of all...the perfect pair of Crystal Pumps!

NOW AVAILABLE!!!

Shorespeare is loosely based on a Midsummer Night's Dream. Shakespeare, with the help of Cupid, has landed at the Jersey Shore. Cupid inspires him to write a play about two New Jersey sweethearts, Cleo and Toni. Shakespeare is put off by their accent and way of talking, but decides to send the two teenagers on a course of true love. Toni and Cleo are determined to get married right after they graduate from high school, but in order to do so they must pass this course of true love that Cupid's pixies create and manipulate. As they travel along the boardwalk at the Jersey Shore, Cleo and Toni, meet a handful of historical figures disguised as the carnies. Confucius teaches Cleo the "Zen of Snoring", Charles Ponzi teaches them the importance of "White Lies", Leonardo Da Vinci shows them the "Art of Multitasking", and finally they meet Napolean who tries to help them to "Accept Shortcomings" of each other. After going through all these lessons, the sweethearts decide that marriage should wait, and Cupid is proud of Shakespeare who has finally reached out to the modern youth.

NOW AVAILABLE!!!

Everyone has heard the phrase, "it's the squeaky wheel that gets the oil," but how many people know the Back-story? The story begins in a kingdom far, far away over the rainbow – a kingdom called Spokend. This kingdom of wheels is a happy one for the gods have blessed the tiny hamlet with plentiful sunshine, water and most important –oil. Until a terrible drought starts to dry up all the oil supplies. What is to be done?

The powerful barons of industry and politicians decide to hold a meeting to decide how to solve the situation. Since Spokend is a democracy all the citizens come to the meeting but their voices are ignored – especially the voice of one of the poorer citizens of the community suffering from a squeak that can only be cured with oil, Spare Wheel and his wife Fifth Wheel. Despite Spare Wheel's desperate pleas for oil, he is ignored and sent home without any help or consideration.

Without oil, Spare Wheel's squeak becomes so bad he loses his job and his family starts to suffer when his sick leave and unemployment benefits run out. What is he to do? Spare Wheel and Fifth Wheel develop a scheme that uses the squeak to their advantage against the town magistrate Big Wheel who finally relents and gives over the oil. Thus, for years after in the town of Spokend citizens in need of help are told "It's the squeaky wheel that gets the oil."

www.ingramcontent.com/pod-product-compliance
Lightning Source LLC
Chambersburg PA
CBHW071311060426
42444CB00034B/1772